MW01142788

Essential Questio..
How do different groups contribute to a cause?

THE VICTORY Garden

by Feana Tu'akoi
illustrated by Seitu Hayden

Chapter 1
Shopping for Spinach

"It's not fair," complained Betty as they left the grocery store. She switched the shopping basket to her other hand and swung it in agitation.

"What's not fair?" her mother asked.

"Rationing," Betty said, rattling the few purchases that the basket held. She knew World War II was on, but she could not stand all the restrictions. "We have more money since Dad enlisted in the army. We should be allowed to buy whatever we want."

Betty's mother sighed as they headed around the corner toward the produce market. "We've been over this already," she said. "With so many workers away at war, the country can't produce as much food as before, and much of what we do produce is needed by the troops. Rationing is a sensible way to ensure everyone gets a fair share."

"Fair share," Betty repeated, fishing out a small packet of sugar from her basket. "We aren't allowed to buy enough sugar to bake the most minuscule cake, so how is that fair?"

"It's fair because everyone gets the same amount," her mother said patiently, "and don't worry, we can still bake that cake because I've been saving up sugar from other weeks."

Betty sighed and dropped the sugar back into the basket. "It's not just the baking," she said. "I'm tired of never having quite enough."

"We have more than enough," her mother said with a laugh. "Don't you remember what it was like during the Depression? When your father was unemployed, we were often hungry, but now we have plenty to eat."

Betty knew she should not grumble, but there were so many things she wanted to have that were not always available. She followed her mother across the street to the produce market, and suddenly, a smile lit up her face. "At least we'll have spinach tonight, and that's my favorite vegetable," she announced happily.

When they reached the market, however, the doors were closed. A sign in the window told everyone to come back on Wednesday when more vegetables would be delivered. Betty was disappointed. "See, I can't even have spinach when I want it."

Betty turned and stomped up the street, but then she saw something that made her pause. Pinned to the board outside the library was a bulletin about victory gardens. It said that planting a victory garden would make household rations stretch further, which started Betty thinking.

"Do you think I could grow spinach?" she asked her mother, pointing to the poster. "Then I would be able to have spinach whenever I wanted, even when the produce market is out."

Betty's mother liked the idea of growing vegetables. During World War I, she'd had a victory garden herself, although it was called a liberty garden back then. She remembered the day her father had cleared a big plot for her on the farm and helped her with the planting.

"That's it, Lillian," her father said, laying down his hoe. "Your liberty garden is ready, and from now on, its survival is up to you."

"Don't worry, I'll do all the weeding and watering," Lillian promised. "My garden will grow healthy and strong."

"Well, you're off to a good start," her father assured her. "You've prepared the soil well, and you've made sure there's diversity by sowing different kinds of seeds."

"I have cabbage, lettuce, tomatoes, corn, and potatoes," Lillian said excitedly. "Soon we'll have all the vegetables we could possibly want!"

"It was exceedingly hard work," Betty's mother explained, "but it made a big difference to our family meals. From then on, we always had plenty of vegetables, and we felt much healthier, too."

"If you could do it, I can do it," Betty said with enthusiasm. "I'm going to plant all kinds of vegetables, not just spinach. We'll have loads of interesting, fresh things to eat, and I'll be helping the war effort!"

Chapter 2
A Garden at School

The following day at lunchtime, Betty told her friends about her garden plans.

"A victory garden is a terrific idea," Dorothy said as they flopped down at the edge of the school's grassy field.

"It sure is, and I'll help you prepare it," Eli offered.

"I will, too," George said, settling himself on the lawn and taking an apple from his pocket, "but where are you going to put it? After all, you live in an apartment without a yard or even a balcony."

"That's the problem," Betty said with a sigh. "Mr. Jefferson, our building superintendent, is building a window box for my spinach, but I don't know where the rest of my garden can go."

"Maybe you could use a vacant lot," Eli said. "My cousin has a victory garden on a lot near his apartment, and he grows enough vegetables for everyone in his building."

Betty considered it. "It's a good idea, but there aren't any empty lots in my neighborhood." She opened her lunch bag and took out a sandwich. "I guess I'll just have to stick with spinach," she added dispiritedly.

There was quiet for a moment while George finished his apple and the other three ate their sandwiches. "It's a shame we can't have a garden here," George commented. "It's exceptionally flat, and it gets plenty of sun."

"That's a fantastic idea," Betty said, her eyes growing wide with excitement. "We should plant a victory garden at school. Come on, let's go ask Mr. Montgomery for permission."

The four friends went inside and explained their idea to their teacher, Mr. Montgomery. He told them that he had his own victory garden at home and thought their idea was great.

"There is one problem, however," Mr. Montgomery added. "As you know, the principal is in the hospital, so I can't ask her permission. I know Mrs. Orwell is very proud of the school's sports program, and the garden will take some of the space away from the practice field. There's a distinct possibility she'll disapprove of the idea."

"Oh, but if we wait until Mrs. Orwell recovers from her operation, the best time for planting might have passed," Betty said, her voice full of disappointment. "We won't be able to have a victory garden until next year."

"Lots of students don't have room for a garden at home," Dorothy added, "and because of the shortages, it can be hard to get enough vegetables. Healthy, well-fed students are really important, don't you think?" she asked earnestly.

"The schoolyard is certainly big enough," Eli added. "We can grow lots of vegetables over by the classrooms and still have plenty of lawn left for sports."

"Plus we'll be helping the war effort, and that's more important than playing sports," George added.

Mr. Montgomery laughed, "Enough! You've already convinced me!" Then his expression turned serious as he said, "But I can give my permission only on one condition— if Mrs. Orwell doesn't like the garden, then we pull out everything with no complaints."

Betty thought for a moment, then said, "I'm willing to take that risk, Mr. Montgomery. This is important to me, and I'm fully committed." The others nodded in agreement.

Chapter 3
Making a Plan

The next morning, Mr. Montgomery told Betty she was allowed to address the school assembly. At first, Betty was nervous speaking in front of the entire student body, but she soon found herself talking passionately about victory gardens and her plan to put one in at school. She also mentioned the possibility that they might have to pull the garden out if Mrs. Orwell disapproved.

"We can grow lots of delicious vegetables," Betty told everyone. "We'll share the work, and we'll share the produce. It'll be satisfying to eat food we've grown ourselves, and it will be much cheaper than buying vegetables at the market."

Most of the students liked the garden idea, and some began to nod approvingly. A few students said they did not want to get involved in case Mrs. Orwell told them to pull the garden out, and one girl said she'd rather grow flowers.

"Flowers would be attractive," Betty agreed diplomatically, "but during a war, we need to concentrate on providing food and other essentials." By the end of the assembly, many recruits had signed up to help.

"We have more than enough workers," Betty told Dorothy as they made their way back to their classroom. "Now all we need is the equipment."

"Don't forget the seeds," Dorothy reminded her. "We need to have something to plant!"

Betty and her friends put a message on the school bulletin board asking for contributions to the garden. Some people loaned them gardening equipment, some gave seeds, and others volunteered their time and labor.

Mr. Montgomery loaned the children a book from the Department of Agriculture called *Victory Gardens*, which he had used when setting up his own garden. It contained lots of great ideas, such as how to get the soil ready and how to plant and look after the seeds. It also told them not to plant too much of one kind of vegetable at once. The idea was to have a continuous supply of a range of vegetables. That way, nothing would be wasted.

The children studied the book's vegetable charts and planting calendar, and then they drew a plan for their own garden. They decided to start by growing tomatoes, beans, lettuce, cabbage, carrots, and onions.

"Plus we'll grow lots of spinach," Betty said. "I can only grow a small amount in my window box, and I don't want to run out!"

When the plan was finished, they asked Mr. Montgomery to look it over in case they had forgotten something important.

Mr. Montgomery studied the plan carefully. "You've done a thorough job," he said, "but I think you should move the tomatoes to the back so they don't block the sunlight from reaching the other vegetables."

Eli grinned as he made the changes to the plan. "We forgot how tall tomato plants can grow," he said. "Thanks, Mr. Montgomery."

Next they checked that they had all the seeds they needed.

"We have everything except tomato seeds," Eli said.

"My grandpa is growing tomato seedlings in trays," Dorothy said. "When they're ready to plant out in his garden, I can intercept him and ask for some. I'm sure he won't mind."

"When do you think they'll be ready?" George asked.

"They're nearly ready now," Dorothy said. "Grandpa's planning to plant them this weekend."

"That's wonderful timing," Betty said. "We'll prepare our garden this weekend, too. At Friday's school assembly, I'll ask everyone to come and help."

"We should invite Mr. Montgomery as well," said George. "Just to watch, not to work, of course."

"Good idea—he can be the guest of honor at our victory garden groundbreaking," Betty said.

Chapter 4
Working Together

On Saturday morning, Betty, Dorothy, Eli, and George arrived early at school to mark out the area for the garden before the helpers arrived.

Dorothy and Eli used twine to mark a huge rectangle on the lawn. They were careful to leave a wide path of grass around the outside.

"That way, people can walk around the garden without disturbing the vegetables," Dorothy said.

Next, George and Betty hammered a wooden stake into each corner, and everyone helped to tie the twine on tightly from stake to stake.

"I see you're already hard at work," called Mr. Montgomery as he approached the garden site. "The shape of your garden looks mathematically perfect."

Betty turned around to greet her teacher but then stopped in surprise. Mr. Montgomery was not wearing his usual suit but was dressed in old overalls, a casual shirt, and a wide-brimmed hat instead.

Mr. Montgomery laughed at her expression. "Did you really think I'd just come to watch?" he asked. "I don't want to miss out on all the action!"

Soon other helpers arrived, many carrying spades, rakes, watering cans, and other gardening equipment.

Betty told them that the first job was to dig out the garden and loosen the soil. Everyone helped to dig around the edges, using the twine to guide them, but it was tough work. The ground was hard and difficult to break up. It took them nearly an hour just to dig the outline of the garden.

Betty shook her head as they removed the twine. "This is more difficult than I had imagined," she told the others. "At this rate, we'll be digging all day and we won't get any planting done."

That was when Mr. Montgomery's son, Robert, arrived, leading a horse that was pulling some machinery.

"Sorry I'm late," Robert called, "but it took a while to get here from the farm. I know how hard the soil is around here, so I brought my horse and plow to help till the ground."

Everyone watched in astonishment as Robert led the horse to the garden area and set up the plow. Slowly and steadily, he walked the horse up and down through the garden plot as the plow churned the ground, leaving lumps of uneven soil piled behind it.

"We really appreciate your help," Betty said when he had finished. "Our work will be so much easier now."

Betty felt relieved that the work was done so quickly, but she was also a little worried. The previously smooth lawn was thoroughly churned up, and there was definitely less room for playing sports. What would Mrs. Orwell say?

The helpers were all busy working, so Betty pushed aside her concerns and joined in. Within an hour, they had the garden dug, raked, and ready for planting.

After a quick lunch break, some people began making furrows for planting, and others followed them spreading the seeds. Then they covered the seeds with soil and sprinkled the ground with water. By the time the garden was finished, they were all dirty and exhausted, but also very proud of themselves.

Just then, a newspaper reporter arrived and approached Mr. Montgomery. "Tell me about your victory garden," he said.

Mr. Montgomery shook his head. "It's not my garden," he said. "I'm just a helper; Betty here is the head of operations."

"So this was your idea, Betty?" the reporter asked.

Betty shook her head, too. "No, I just wanted my own victory garden. George came up with the idea of growing one at school."

"We all worked on it together," George said with a shy smile.

By the time they finished telling their story, the reporter had written pages of notes and was ready to take a photograph.

Everyone lined up and beamed at him, but just as he clicked the camera, a voice cried out, "Stop, stop!"

It was Mrs. Orwell in a wheelchair being pushed toward them by her husband. The four friends looked anxiously at one another.

"I've just heard what's happening," Mrs. Orwell said. "What were you all thinking?" she demanded. The children exchanged glances again, and Betty felt her stomach tying itself in a knot.

Mrs. Orwell continued, "How could you possibly think I would allow … this reporter to leave without my telling him how very proud I am of all of you?" she finished with a beaming smile. "Betty and all of you helpers, may your marvelous victory garden help bring victory to us all!"

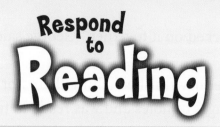

Respond to Reading

Summarize

Use the most important details from *The Victory Garden* to summarize the story. Your graphic organizer may help you.

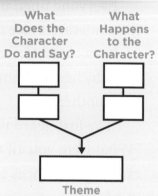

What Does the Character Do and Say?	What Happens to the Character?

Theme

Text Evidence

1. What features of the text help you identify it as historical fiction? **GENRE**

2. What is the "cause" in *The Victory Garden*? What group contributed to that cause? What did the group do? **THEME**

3. On page 2, the word *fair* sounds the same as the word *fare*, but they have different meanings. What is the meaning of *fair*? Use context clues to help you. Then find three other pairs of homophones in the story. **HOMOPHONES**

4. Betty and her friends give reasons for making a victory garden at school. Write about the points they made. How does including these reasons help communicate the story's theme? **WRITE ABOUT READING**

Compare Texts
Read about how victory gardens helped the
United States during World War II.

Gardening for
UNCLE SAM

During World War II, a lot of food was needed for the
armed forces. Labor and transportation shortages made
food harder to produce and move around the country.

To make sure everyone had enough food to eat, the
government introduced rationing and asked Americans to
plant vegetable gardens. Posters, films, newspapers, and
magazines urged people to garden wherever they could.
People replaced lawns and flower beds with vegetable
beds. Gardening was a way ordinary people could do their
part for the war effort. It was seen as a patriotic duty, and
the gardens became known as victory gardens.

Home Gardens in World War I

The victory gardens of
World War II were not
a new idea. During
World War I, the U.S.
government encouraged
people to plant vegetable
gardens, which were known
as liberty gardens.

PLANT A VICTORY GARDEN

OUR FOOD
IS FIGHTING

A GARDEN WILL MAKE YOUR RATIONS GO FURTHER

17

When victory gardens were first promoted, many people did not know much about gardening, so the United States Department of Agriculture published booklets to provide advice. *Victory Gardens*, published in 1942, taught readers about soil preparation, planting, cultivation, and harvesting. It even gave advice on how the vegetables could be cooked.

Victory gardens started appearing all over the country. In cities, people grew them wherever land was available, such as in window boxes, in containers on balconies and rooftops, and in vacant lots, playgrounds, schoolyards, and city parks. In 1943, First Lady Eleanor Roosevelt planted a victory garden at the White House.

The U.S government helped citizens learn about gardening, promoting it as a way for them to support the war effort.

Some people planted individual victory gardens to provide food for their own families, while others contributed to community gardens. Many people grew more than they needed and shared the extra with others in their neighborhoods. Doing so helped them feel they were doing their part to help the United States win the war.

The victory garden campaign was very successful. Approximately 20 million victory gardens were planted in the United States during World War II, and they produced more than 40 percent of the nation's fruits and vegetables. People's diets vastly improved because of this, and there was more food available to send to the troops, too. By planting victory gardens, the American people made a significant contribution to the war effort.

Make Connections

Why were victory gardens needed during World War II? How did the people who planted them help the war cause? ESSENTIAL QUESTION

Using examples from *The Victory Garden* and *Gardening for Uncle Sam*, explain why people were prepared to work hard to plant their own victory gardens. TEXT TO TEXT

Focus on
Literary Elements

Flashbacks Flashbacks can be used in both fiction and nonfiction. They are parts of a text that tell what happened in a time earlier than when the main story or article occurs. Flashbacks can provide background about a character or event. The writer often lets the reader know that the story is about to go back in time by having a character pause to retell or recall events from the past. A flashback can be long or short. It can be a separate chapter, or it can be part of the main text.

Read and Find On page 4, Betty's mother remembers her childhood and the vegetable garden her father helped her make. The flashback is told as if it happening in the "present" (actually a time between 1916 and 1918). At the end of the flashback, the writer brings us back to the time period of the main narrative.

Your Turn

Think about Betty and the garden she helps organize at her school. She would be very old if she were alive today. How might she reflect on her garden and the food she and her school friends grew? Write a short flashback from Betty's point of view, describing how she felt about her contribution to the war effort.